GOD'S
BLUEPRINT
for a
HAPPY
HOME

What God says about . . .
Marriage
Living Together
Divorce
Infidelity
Reconciliation

Published by Straight Talk Books
P.O. Box 301, Milwaukee, WI 53201
800.661.3311 · timeofgrace.org

Printed in the United States of America
ISBN: 978-1-949488-79-1

Contents

Introduction

When an older friend told me about his epic anniversary party, I knew I needed to hear the whole story. He and his wife decided to go big after being together for 50 years, so they threw a multigenerational marriage celebration. They spent an entire week together—eating, talking, swimming, hiking—and toasted to five decades of love. At the same time, their children celebrated 25 years of marriage, 23 years of marriage, 20 years of marriage, and 10 years of marriage, a total of 128 years of commitment. But, even better, was that at the start and end of every day of their celebration was Jesus. Every morning, one of their sons led their entire family in worshiping Jesus. Every evening, one of the grandchildren led them in praying to that same Savior.

#relationshipgoals! Isn't that incredible? That isn't some made-up story. That happened in real life. My friend would tell you (emphatically) that he is a sinner, that he and his wife are far from perfect, but I bet you would agree with me that they seem to be a happy, holy family.

Isn't that what we all want? Whether you are married, hope to be married, or just love people who are married, we all want happy homes. We want to get as close to happily ever after as possible. And for those of us who follow Jesus, we want to be holy too. We want to follow God's plan for relationships, doing what he says is good for our souls. In other words, we want a happy, holy home.

But I bet you know that my friend's story is not normal. Some relationships (many relationships?) are less happy and holy and more sad and sinful. Maybe your parents' relationship was like that. Maybe you've been in a relationship like that. Maybe you are in a relationship like that. You might be married but, honestly, not happily married, and you don't know how to get unstuck. Maybe you hope to be married, but you're scared that something will go wrong. Maybe you're living with your partner. Grandma is freaking out, but you need to know if you're compatible before you say, "I do." Maybe you're one of the many couples from my church who is trying to heal from infidelity, to rebuild what sin wrecked and, maybe, build something even better than before. Or maybe you just know people in those same situations, and you aren't sure how to help your friend's marriage or your brother who is living with his girlfriend or your sister who just told you about her affair. Whatever your relationship status, I bet you want the relationships around you to be happy and holy.

And that's why I'm super glad you are reading this book, because we're going to open the pages of the Bible to see how our heavenly Father can get us closer to happy and holy and help us avoid the sad and sinful. We'll cover God's amazing blueprint for marriage but also see what he says about infidelity and divorce. No matter what the topic, we'll find that God is with us through it all and his plans and guidance and promises are so, so good.

Living Together Before Marriage?

OK, I know. This is supposed to be a book about marriage and happy homes, but please bear with me, because it seems to me that a chapter talking about living together before marriage is a good idea. Here's why. I once forced a room full of pastors and ministry leaders to take a theological stand on one of the more personal issues of modern times. I began, "On the count of three, I want you to vote for option 1 or option 2, and those are your only two options. Option 1—Living together before marriage is wrong no matter what. No matter what a couple does or doesn't do under the same roof, sharing an address before marriage is sinful. Option 2—Living together before marriage isn't essentially wrong. You may or may not do wrong things while living together, but the very act of sharing an address is okay with Jesus. Ready to vote? Three, two, one, go!"

The answers that followed were interesting. The

debate that followed the answers was even more so.

But no matter the vote, we all realized that living together before marriage is something we needed to figure out, because it has become, in just a few generations, the new normal, even in the church. And that debate—Is it wrong? Is it right? Does it depend?—is happening all the time among families and friends and fellow Christians.

I am not sure about you, but the longer I live and the more couples I see, both healthy and dysfunctional, the more I realize why living together is such an emotionally charged issue. Marriage is meant to be forever, so it's important to know, as best you can, if you two are meant to share a marriage. How will you two do sharing a house, a bathroom, a budget? Divorces happen every day because of money, sexual compatibility, and day-to-day doing life together. So, many would claim, it only makes sense to spend some days living together before taking those sacred vows.

Add to that all the failed marriages many of us have seen, often up close and painfully personal. Grandma might scold you for "shacking up" with your boyfriend, but after watching your parents argue for years until their separation, you are terrified to jump into marriage and end up in the same sad situation.

Add to that the crazy cost of rent, the inconvenience of driving back to your apartment every night, and the simple fact that you love each other and love being with each other, and you see why, in so many ways, living together seems to make sense. It seems reasonable.

If you are in love and love God, there are two questions you need to answer in regard to this issue. First, will living together make you happy? Second, does God see living together as holy? If your goal is to have a happy, holy home, you need to know the Bible's answers to those crucial questions, so let's explore them here.

Part 1—Does living together make couples happy? Let's step back, look at the data, and ask, "Does living together make us better, stronger, and happier as couples? Is it good for relationships? Good for children?"

No one can deny that there are some real benefits to cohabitation (that's the fancy word for living together before marriage). If you have extra time and money for each other and for others because you're not paying two rents, cleaning two places, etc., that's a point in the happiness column. Every couple knows that investing time and energy into your relationship is the fuel that makes a good relationship run, and cohabitation seems to give you just that.

Plus, living together lets you know what you're getting into! As most reality shows show us, you get to know the real version of someone when the cameras are always rolling. They can't hide their flaws and less flattering qualities. In the same way, when you start and end your day with each other, there is little that you can hide. Sharing the same space gives you a chance to know each other like never before, allowing you to take your marriage vows with open eyes (or decide to call things off before the big day).

No wonder a 2019 study of 18- to 49-year-olds revealed that for every one person who thinks that living together is bad, five to six believe that it is good.[1] I wouldn't be surprised if you were persuaded to join that majority because of the pros listed previously.

But what about the cons? What about the big picture? Wise people aren't persuaded by one side of an argument, so what speaks against the wisdom of moving in before marriage?

One of the helpful parts about living in the 2020s is that we have a truckload of in-depth studies on this issue, and the data, surprisingly, is quite one-sided. According to the latest research, couples who marry without living together trust each other more, serve each other more, are more satisfied with household chores, and are more satisfied with their sex lives.[2]

Those who marry without living together first are more likely to be faithful to each other.

Those who marry without living together first are more likely to be faithful to each other, more likely to stay together, and more likely to raise healthy children—three outcomes on the top of our list of relationship goals.

If you or someone you love is living with their partner pre-vows, take a second to reread the last two paragraphs and underline the cons of cohabitation. Without foolishly assuming that you will be the exception to the rule (that's what fools do, according to the book of Proverbs), honestly ask yourself if that is the kind of relationship you prefer. Notice words like *significantly* and *robust*. Is that risk worth saving a few thousand in rent or a few hours of travel each week?

But while you are comparing the pros and the cons, you should wonder why. Why would living together first and getting to know each other better lead to a less satisfying life? That almost feels illogical, doesn't it?

But there is a logical, biblical explanation. Living together might look a lot like an unofficial marriage, but it is missing the most important part—the vow. When you live together, you have not taken a vow. You have not made a promise to your partner. You have not bound yourself to better behavior. In fact, you might be doing just the opposite.

When you live together before marriage, you are teaching yourself to see your relationship in a way that violates the essence of marriage. Like a basketball player who practices with bad form and then hopes to jump into a real game, cohabitation is not a paperless version of marriage but a dangerous distortion of it.

What do I mean? Here's what God says about marriage: **"Each one of you also must love his wife as he loves himself, and the wife must respect her husband"** (Ephesians 5:33). Notice what word isn't in this verse— *If.* Marriage isn't, "I love you, but if I'm not happy, then

I'm moving out." It's not, "I love you, but if you don't do enough for me, I'm packing up my stuff." No. The vow of marriage is not, "I will if" but simply, "I will." I will love you (period). If you deserve my love, I will love you. If you don't deserve my love, I will love you. Or, as the classic vow states it, I will love you "for better or for worse." Marriage is unconditional love with no ifs or asterisks, a vow to be together until death do us part.

But that's not living together. Living together comes with a thousand ifs and zero vows. Living together leaves the door unlocked, giving you a chance to leave whenever you want to. And that trains you to treat marriage like a contract and not a covenant.

No wonder couples who cohabitate end up divorced more often. They have hundreds, perhaps thousands, of days of practicing the thought, "I can leave if I am un-happy." That's why the wisdom of the church has urged couples over the years, "Wait! If you want to be happy, wait." While it won't be convenient, the wait is worth it.

When I was a young pastor, I was teaching a middle school Bible class when one of our students brought one of his friends as a guest for the very first time. That particular class was about sex and marriage (of course . . .), so I opened the Scriptures and tried to teach God's view on such issues faithfully. That's when the young guest raised his hand. Uh-oh.

But I shouldn't have been worried. Because instead of asking a question or questioning my doctrine, this teenage boy simply made a statement—"Pastor, the world would be better if everyone did that. There would be no families who don't have dads around and no people having kids before they're ready."

Wow. He wasn't talking about biblical morality. He was just talking about being happy. He was talking about family and stability. This young man hadn't read all the studies about the pros and cons of cohabitation. Instead, he just reacted based on his own experiences and said, "God's way seems way better."

Does doing our own thing with sex and marriage make us long-term happier? No. The risks outweigh the rewards. Thus, studies and scriptural wisdom say, "If you want to be happy, wait until you're married."

But what about the holy? That's the second question we need to cover here. Because if you are wired at all like I am, you know the difference between a probability and a prohibition. If I was living together with my girlfriend and taking this message to heart, I might push back, "Okay, I hear what you're saying. We are more likely to have issues if we live together, but answer this question—Is it wrong? Is there a passage where God says it is sin? If we try to remember what you said about the vows and 'no ifs and asterisks,' can we live under the same roof and still love God?" Those are fair questions. God gags when we add to or subtract from his Word, when customs and traditions are treated like chapters and verses, so can Christians say that the Word of Christ forbids cohabitation?

I'll be straight with you. In the entire Bible, there isn't a verse that says, "You shall not live together."

But there is a verse that deserves our full consideration: **"Marriage should be honored by all, and the marriage bed kept pure, for God will judge the adulterer and all the sexually immoral"** (Hebrews 13:4). Let's break that down and see how it applies to our questions.

"Marriage should be honored by all." Who should honor marriage? All of us. If your parents were happily married or bitterly divorced, you should honor marriage. If you yourself have been divorced, you should honor marriage. If you two are still in school and living off ramen and water, you should honor marriage. If you two are older and living off of social security benefits, you should honor marriage. Marriage should be honored by *all*.

Every so often, I hear someone say, "Marriage is just a piece of paper." Hebrews 13:4 forbids such a view. Marriage is not a piece of paper but rather one of God's first ideas. It shows up on page one of the Bible and is a frequent theme in the teaching of Jesus himself. The Bible honors marriage. We all should too.

The Bible honors marriage. We all should too.

"And the married bed kept pure." Not only did God give us marriage; he gave us the marriage bed. Sex was God's idea! God invented sex, smiled, and said to Adam and Eve, "You're welcome." And God, who loves every person he has every created, has put a sign on the bedroom door—Reserved for marriage.

In God's eyes, sex is a marriage thing. Sexual pleasure is a marriage thing. The joy and creativity and pleasure that make sex good are for a husband and wife to explore together under the protective roof of their lifelong vows.

If you wonder why God reserves sex strictly for marriage, I encourage you to go to timeofgrace.store and search for a book I wrote called *Sexpectations*, which explores the wisdom of being both excited and strict about sexual morality. But for now, note the clear words of Hebrews chapter 13: the marriage bed (a.k.a. sex) should be kept pure.

"For God will judge the adulterer and all the sexually immoral." Apparently, the marriage bed is not a joke to God. He doesn't laugh when singles sneak into that reserved room. He doesn't wink when one thing leads to another with vowless couples. If you're living together and sleeping together, let that sink in. God will judge all the sexually immoral. Not might. He will. He will not judge some. He will judge all. Sex before marriage is sin, as serious to God as racism or child abuse is to you.

So if you just shrug and say, "Whatever," if you go back to that same bed and do those same things, if you pressure her into moving into your house or seduce him into climbing into your bed, if you stay sexually active without any remorse or repentance, God will judge you.

That is my concern. If you live together, you won't be holy. If you share the same bed, you won't keep it pure. I doubt I'm wrong. I didn't live with my wife, Kim, until after our wedding night, but we still struggled to honor God's boundaries for our bodies. When you love someone in every way and are physically attracted to them every day, who can resist? Be real with me right now. Can you share the same bed, bedroom, and bathroom and remain pure? Can you be right there when he gets out of the shower or she puts on her bra and yet remain self-controlled and holy?

No, there is no passage that bluntly says, "Thou shall not cohabitate," but there is this: "God will judge the sexually immoral."

I imagine you might be mad right now because I'm messing with your plan. You planned to live together and save money so you could have your dream wedding, and now I'm throwing a holy wrench right into your spokes. I bet this could cause a fight if you bring it up. You feel convicted, but he doesn't care. You know, deep down, that you are disobeying God, but she isn't bothered by these words. This message might mess with your relationship. But listen—I would rather mess with your sex than lose your soul.

You might even have a decision to make. Maybe that means moving out because you love God more than the money or the convenience. Maybe it means getting married sooner rather than later, even if the wedding isn't what you dreamed about as a little girl. Maybe you get married now and have a big party in two years, something that my church does with couples all the time. I'm not sure what step you will take, but I do know you should wait. That's what people who are pursuing holiness do.

Remember the teenage kid who came to my Bible class? After I got done teaching about sex, marriage, and living together, he raised his hand again, this time not with his perspective but with a direct question. "Pastor Mike, do you keep all these commandments? Loving your wife, waiting for marriage, not lusting with your eyes, all the stuff you just taught us. Do you do all that?"

Ugh. You might know that my sexual history has not been spotless. Kim and I were both virgins until our wedding night, but there are other ways to be sexually immoral, and I was. Hebrews claimed that God will judge "all" the sexually immoral, which includes men like me. So what do I do? What do we do?

Answer—We run to Jesus. We run to Jesus in repentance. We cling to the cross and make our confession, "We sinned. Jesus, we sinned so many times. We are sorry." Like the prodigal son in Jesus' story, we say to our partner, **"I have sinned against heaven and against you"** (Luke 15:21). We confess that we loved convenience more than Jesus, money more than our Maker, our wants more than God's will. No blaming it on our parents' ugly divorce. No excusing it on our tight budget. We simply own it. We repent.

Jesus opens his arms to us.

And (this is my favorite part) Jesus forgives us. He opens his arms to us, to all of us who come to him broken and remorseful. Your situation might be as sinful as the prostitutes who gathered around Jesus or the woman caught in the act of adultery or the countless sinners who cried out to Jesus for mercy. But Jesus' reaction to you is the same as it was toward them. He loved them. He cleansed them. He saved them.

Just like the father loved his prodigal son. When that sexually sinful kid finally came home with nothing to offer his father but his confession, the father saw him (because he was waiting for him), ran to him, hugged and kissed him, forgave him, clothed him, cleansed him, wrapped his arms around him, and threw a party in his honor. That's what our God is like to sexual sinners who come back to him.

You might be living with your girlfriend right now and finally realizing your sin. Or perhaps you're thinking back to how your marriage began—out of order and far from holy. But Hebrews chapter 13 tells us that the Jesus who forgave sinners two thousand years ago is still at it today: **"Jesus Christ is the same yesterday and today and forever"** (verse 8). Jesus has not changed. The same Savior who opened his arms to messy souls is opening them to you and me. The cross of Jesus doesn't have an expiration date! We run to him again and again and again and again, and the blood that he shed makes us clean. It makes us pure. It makes us enough for God. This is why we love God. This is why we trust God.

The five pastors at my church, in our one hundred total years of ministry, have probably officiated a thousand weddings. Church weddings, barn weddings, beach weddings, all the weddings. We've heard more "I dos" and eaten more fried chicken than you can imagine. But do you know the weddings we've loved the most? Not the ones with the designer dresses (although a beaming bride is beautiful). Or the late-night pizza bars (although I do adore that recent invention). No, the weddings we love the most are the weddings where God is loved the most. Where a man and his wife love each other a lot but love Jesus even more. Where their lives say, "Father, not our will but your will be done."

So if you are living together or thinking about living together or know someone who is living together, remember this: a couple that puts Jesus first, no matter how hard that choice may be, creates the happiest, holiest home.

Study Questions

1. Go back to God's creation of marriage in Genesis 2:18–25. What does verse 24 have to say about the beauty of intimacy and the commitment of marriage?

2. Agree/Disagree: Christian friends should say something to Christian friends who are living together.

3. "Where sin increased, grace increased all the more" (Romans 5:20). Why is this verse so important as many of us think about our personal history with relationships?

Unique and United

We can't start a discussion about happy homes and marriages without talking about the differences between men and women, right? God created two different genders for a reason. Yet it seems we are in the middle of a gender crisis. Just ask Gillette. In early 2019, the shaving company released a commercial that challenged men to be better. Better it implied than their groping, harassing, belittling, and bullying past. Within just four months, the commercial had over 30M YouTube views and more than 700,000 likes . . . and more than 1.4M dislikes.[3] Many believed the commercial overcorrected and emasculated men altogether.

USA Today commented on that tension, calling it a boyhood "crisis." A culture where boys don't know what it means to be a man. Where the men they see at home and online are the ugly extremes—the physically aggressive, emotionally abusive, alpha male or the pathetically passive, conversationally evasive man who has no plans for his family, no goals for his faith, no leadership in his church, no love for his home. One podcaster I know frequently asks young men what it means to be a man. They have no clue.

But this crisis isn't just among men. It affects women too. In the last century, so many doors have opened for women (thank God), but the bar has been raised to an almost unreachable level. Now you have to go to college and maybe grad school, establish your career, sell essential oils on the side, stay connected to your tribe, find a guy and get him to commit, start a family and find a day care, practice self-care, and . . . and . . . and. It's okay for women to admit they're kind of a mess, but which word most often comes before mess? *Hot.* Because women still have to look good while doing all that.

And the crisis affects men and women together in their homes. What do good husbands do these days? and wives? Is there any difference? Are spouses interchangeable parts? Does gender even matter to Jesus? As we raise our sons and daughters, what do we tell them about their roles and their goals? The answers to those questions are more passionate than the comments section on the Gillette ad.

Let's start at the beginning. Literally. The very first pages of Genesis lay a foundation for everything the Bible says about gender. Let me give you the big idea up front. Ready for it? God made men and women *unique* and *united*. Before there was sin or chauvinism or selfishness, God himself made men and women unique and united.

Let me prove it from Genesis chapter 1:

So God created mankind in his own image, in the image of God he created them; male and female he created them. God blessed them and said to them, "Be fruitful and increase in number; fill the earth and subdue it. Rule over the fish in the sea and the birds in the sky and over every living creature that moves on the ground." (verses 27,28)

Let's focus on a few truths from these verses . . .

First, men and women are *united in God's image.* "In the image of God he created them." This is the highest compliment God could ever give us. We weren't created with his height or his hair but with his holiness. His perfection. His sinlessness. That's what God's image is, to be like God spiritually. This single verse should make *sexist Christians* an oxymoron. Any chauvinistic stereotype about women or degrading joke about men cannot get Genesis 1:27 to laugh. You can't degrade someone who is in the A+ image of our holy God. What united the man and the

Through Jesus, our identity is in his image.

woman then is what unites all God's sons and daughters now. Through Jesus, our identity is in his image.

Second, men and women are *united in God's mission.* Don't miss this: God said to them, "Subdue [the earth]. Rule over [it]." God said that to . . . *them.* Not just to him but to them. Guys, you rule. Girls, you do too. Together we have this amazing mission from God to rule over the earth, to take whatever is in our care and rule it, organize it, and manage it for the glory of God. Our homes, our gardens, our cities, our churches, our kids, our world. We are called to rule it all for the glory of God. That's our united mission.

But there are some unique things in these verses too. "Male and female he created them." *Men and women are physically unique.* More than ever, science is showing us that truth. From the XX or XY in our chromosomes to the types and amounts of hormones that pump through our bodies to where we store fat to how much skeletal muscle we have, we are unique.

A 2017 *Stanford Medicine* article revealed, "Women excel in several measures of verbal ability—pretty much all of them. . . . Women's reading comprehension and writing ability consistently exceed that of men."[4] But men excel in other ways, both mentally and physically. YouTube "Top 10 Dunks" and you'll see what I mean. Female basketball star Brittney Griner has a 7'2" wingspan, just one inch short of Bucks star Giannis Antetokounmpo. WNBA player Breanna Stewart has a wingspan of 7'1", which is an inch longer than LeBron James' 7'0", but they don't dunk the same. Why can Brittney and Breanna barely two-hand dunk while Giannis and LeBron can fly over 7-footers and murder the rim? Because they're unique. God made men bigger, faster, and stronger. (Of course, there are exceptions. I once came "this" close to losing an arm wrestling match to a petite female friend who was still recovering from having her baby! And, on the average car ride, I speak 12 times more words than my wife does.) But the stereotypes are rooted in science and Scripture. Men and women are unique.

There's more. God said to them, "Be fruitful." *Men and women are sexually unique.* Our body parts are unique. To be fruitful, men and women have unique roles. They unite in sex, but his unique sperm and her unique egg take their unique DNA and make one united baby. Think of the connection between the words *gender*, *genitals*, and *generations*. God said all that in Genesis chapter 1.

And he kept going in Genesis chapter 2:

But for Adam no suitable helper was found. So the Lord God caused the man to fall into a deep sleep; and while he was sleeping, he took one of the man's ribs and then closed up the place with flesh. Then the Lord God made a woman from the rib he had taken out of the man, and he brought her to the man. (verses 20-22)

I know that sounds weird, but this is really important. Because this is the divine definition of being a man or a woman. *Men and women are uniquely called.*

To God, men are like ribs. Poke your ribs once and think of what they do. Ribs are strong. Solid. Protective.

Ribs protect the vital (note that word) and vulnerable (note that word) parts of your body. Ribs stand in between internal organs and outside threats. Ribs take the hit and get bruised so that what we need to live—our hearts, our lungs—stays safe. This, guys, is what it means to be men. God doesn't say much about being a "man's man"— about hunting, fishing, car fixing, truck driving, beard growing—but he does say a lot about being like a rib. About being strong. About taking the hit. About leading for the sake of protecting.

Just think what happens in history or in our own homes when men do this (or they don't). What happens to women and children when men are either aggressive or absent? When they snap and attack the heart of a woman? Or when they bail and leave their kids unprotected? Or when guys at work or on the playground stop protecting each other? Here's what happens: people get hurt. But what happens when men are like ribs? When they stick to their commitments? When they are dependable, reliable, strong? When they stand up for what's right and good and godly? When they use the God-given strength in their bones to serve and protect? Here's what happens: Women and children thrive. They feel safe. They can become everything God created them to be. If you're a guy, keep reading. In later chapters of this book, I will talk about how God challenges and empowers you to embrace what he meant when he made you a man.

If you are a woman, your calling is unique but essential. God called the first woman a "helper suitable for" her man. Now don't look down on that word—*helper*. This isn't like "the help." This is the Hebrew word that's usually used for God. God is an ever-present help in trouble, and our Father knows men need help. To be strong is hard, and men need help. To be selfless is hard, and men need help. To love like Jesus loves and sacrifice like Jesus sacrificed is so hard, and men need help. So God made you. A helper suitable for him.

Because without your vital part, men are just a bunch of dry ribs. The old saying is right, "Behind every good man is a good woman." Behind every good man is a good woman who helped him, who gave him perspective, who supplied him wisdom, who reminded him of his calling, who encouraged him, who put courage in him. Ladies, men can out lift you, but they can't live without you. And in the beginning, God knew it. The dogs and cats and pets were not suitable. That's why he made you, a helper suitable for him.

Put it all together, and what do we have? We have men and women who in a perfect, sinless world were wonderfully united and powerfully unique. And, according to Genesis, God said that it was so good.

So what happened? Why this crisis, this tension, this men vs. women mess that we're in? That answer is in the beginning too. Genesis chapter 3 is sometimes called "the fall," and that's where God's design for us fell apart.

It's the odd story where the devil disguised himself

and tricked God's children. Notice these snippets from that tragic day: **"The serpent said to the woman. . . . The woman said to the serpent. . . . The serpent said to the woman. . . . When the woman saw . . . she took some and ate it"** (verses 1-6). He said, she said, he said, she saw, and she took. Who's missing in that story? Her man. And her God. But there's a twist. Here's what happened next: **"She also gave some to her husband, who was with her, and he ate it"** (verse 6). What? He was with her? While the devil deceived his wife and tried to corrupt her heart with sin, he just stood there? Yes, sir. He just stood there. He had no words. No plans. No protection. He sat there with a remote in his hand while his wife and the whole world fell apart.

In this story we find the *unique temptations* that men and women often face. Men have always been tempted to be either abusive or absent. This is what too often happens in homes and churches. Men just sit there. Men want to be the quarterback on the field, the soldier in the war, the hero in the office, but at home and with church they just sit there. Men don't have a plan. Guys, women love a plan and a guy who has goals. You think they want a six-pack, but they'd rather have a man with six goals for his family. But like the first man, we sons of Adam repeat his sin and fail to lead lovingly and protect those in our care.

But women are tempted too. Tempted to be like Eve, to dismiss their need for protection, to define strength as independence. But every girl who didn't have a good dad knows it's not that simple. You are a vital part of creation, ladies, like the human heart, but you are vulnerable. You will get hurt without help.

The first man and woman *united in their sin* and tried to hide from the holy God. They united in pointing fingers, in blaming others. They *united in their brokenness,* falling far from the image of God. And *God gave them unique consequences.* She would feel the pain of being "fruitful." Kids would be costly. And, God said, she would desire a man like God, but man would

You are a vital part of creation.

rule over her like she was his pet and not his prize. The world would now be filled with more "rulers" than ribs. For him, the consequence would be work, hard work. The soil wouldn't produce fruit easily. The economy would struggle. The salary wouldn't be enough. Work would be filled with thorns, thistles, bosses who don't listen, and employees who won't follow. We feel this, right? We live in a fallen world, where people are not holy like God, where family and work can break our hearts.

But there's one last thing I want you to see in the beginning, one final thing that united Adam and Eve and still unites us today. It's what God said to the serpent: **"I will put enmity between you and the woman, and between your offspring and hers; he will crush your head, and you will strike his heel"** (Genesis 3:15). One day, God promised, Eve's offspring would come, a man born of a woman. He would get hurt; the devil would somehow strike his heel. But at the same time, that "he" would crush the devil's head. He would crush sin. He could crush hell. He would destroy that distance between us and God. This is the very first promise of Jesus. The male born of mother Mary. The Savior who suffered when nails were pounded through his hands and feet. The Jesus who crushed the devil so that everyone who trusts in God would not be crushed but saved. Jesus is the epitome of a man, the ultimate rib who was bruised so we could be blessed, who took the hit so we could be safe in heaven. This is the ultimate thing that unites us all—*Jesus*.

Jesus is where the first humans found their hope. You can too. When you realize you've missed this or messed it up, you can find hope in Jesus. Because God so loved the world—all 3.97 billion males and 3.9 billion females, all the boys and the girls, all the men and the women, you— that he gave Jesus, his only Son, that whoever believes in him—whoever—would have forever life with God. There is one Jesus, one cross, one empty tomb that unites us all in worship and praise. And men might sing bass and women soprano, but we unite our voices to praise the name of Jesus.

In the beginning God made men and women unique. And when things fell apart, he promised his Son, Jesus, to unite us again in love and respect, as protective ribs and helping hearts, as brothers and sisters with one Father.

Study Questions

1. Think of the men from your past (father, brothers, friends, boyfriends, husband, etc.) and consider how safe they made you feel. Were the best protectors the best men?

2. Read Philippians 2:5-11. Why is Jesus the greatest man of all time?

3. Challenge: Men, how could you better protect, emotionally and physically, the people God has put in your life? Women, in what ways could you imitate God, the ultimate Helper, and help those in your circle of influence?

The Point of Marriage

Do you know the Disney movie *Beauty and the Beast*? Even if you haven't seen it, I bet you can guess the plot. Guy meets girl (okay, guy cursed with abnormal amount of body hair meets girl). Guy falls in love with girl. Guy and girl live happily ever after. That's a common script, right? The Beast and Belle. Aladdin and Jasmine. Shrek and Fiona. Eric and Ariel. These movie characters follow the same story. You have to meet your one, fall in love, and then live happily ever after.

But if that's what it takes to be happy, what about the rest of us? What about guy meets girl, girl isn't interested in guy, guy is 35 and single? What about guy meets girl, guy falls in love with girl, after two years guy is scared to commit to girl? What about guy meets girl, guy marries girl, girl's not happy and divorces guy? What about guy meets girl, guy marries girl, guy wonders if he would be happier with another girl? What about girl never meets the right guy? What about you?

We live in a culture with this script—you have to meet the one and fall in love to live happily ever after. But what if that script is actually hurting our happiness? Causing us to date the wrong people for the wrong reasons? Leading us to pressure our single friends into more blind dates? Tricking us into building our marriages on the wrong foundation? Setting us up to get divorced more often? Making us forget about God? What if God had a better script for his single sons, his dating daughters, his married and divorced children? That's what happily ever after is about. How can God bless us, no matter what our relationship status, with contentment, joy, happiness?

Few things have changed as much in American culture as the connection between happiness and marriage. In 1960, 68% of people in their 20s were married. By 2008, that number plummeted to 26%. For the first time in history, the typical American spent more time single than married. Why do you think that is? Why are more and more of us convinced marriage isn't all our grandparents believed, maybe little more than a piece of paper from the clerk of courts?

Could it be the heartbreaking divorces we've experienced or witnessed? Or the cultural shift in accepting sex and living together apart from marriage? Maybe. But I suspect there's something deeper, something more foundational. I think we've forgotten the point of marriage. The original design. God's blueprint.

So I want to bring you to the blueprint, to the

Scripture Jesus and the apostle Paul quoted when asked about marriage. Let's go back to the beginning like we did in the previous chapter to where marriage first started in Genesis chapter 2:

> **Now the Lord God had planted a garden in the east, in Eden; and there he put the man he had formed. The Lord God made all kinds of trees grow out of the ground—trees that were pleasing to the eye and good for food. In the middle of the garden were the tree of life and the tree of the knowledge of good and evil.**
>
> **The Lord God took the man and put him in the Garden of Eden to work it and take care of it."** (verses 8,9,15)

In the beginning, it wasn't Adam and Eve; it was Adam and Eden. A guy and a garden. Eden seems to come from a word that means "luxury" or "delight," and it was the luxurious, delightful place where the first man worshiped. Because that's what Adam's work was. He worshiped God whenever he worked. That was Adam's calling: to worship God with a hard day's work.

But there's more: **"The Lord God commanded the man, 'You are free to eat from any tree in the garden; but you must not eat from the tree of the knowledge of good and evil, for when you eat from it you will certainly** die'" (verses 16,17). Why would God plop some forbidden fruit right in front of Adam's face? Here's what the reformer Martin Luther said about it. He said that God put that forbidden fruit there so Adam could worship. Every time Adam saw the tree and walked past it, he worshiped. He confessed, "I believe God is good. I believe God loves me. I believe God only forbids what would hurt me because God is good." So whether he was working on the trees or walking past that tree, Adam was worshiping.

And he was happy. Because that's what happens when you're hanging out with a good God, when you're in his presence. Which is why God warned, "If you eat that fruit, you will know evil and you will die." *To die* means "to separate" (like physical death separates body and soul). "Adam, if you eat that, you'll be separate from me, different. You won't be holy. You'll hide from me, and I'm the one who makes you happy." You see, sin would lead to sadness. So God told Adam, "Don't sin. Stay with me, and you'll be happy for ever and ever."

But did you notice something about these words? God was speaking these life-changing words about sin and death to Adam. Before Eve was even on the scene, God spoke to Adam, to the husband. God created Adam first and then commanded Adam first, implying Adam would be the one to share God's words with his wife. Adam became the first pastor, the first worship leader, the first husband to turn his home into a house of God.

And that is the blueprint. A husband's calling is to

lead his wife to live happily ever after in the presence of God. I'll write it this way—A husband's call is to lead his wife to the happiest life. You've heard "happy wife, happy life." It's true. Not by just saying, "Yes, dear. You're right, dear." Yuck! What a patronizing, emasculating model for marriage. No, but by passionately leading her to God. Because the most satisfying,

A husband's calling is to lead his wife.

longest lasting happiness is found in God. Every husband's call is to lead his wife to the happiest life, a life close to God.

I wonder how many husbands believe that blueprint. How many of them see a husband's role as providing for his wife's happiness by leading her to God?

Because the temptation is always there, isn't it? To look for happily ever after anywhere but God. That's what the devil did in Eden. And that's what he does today. He tempts men to sit back spiritually, to be passionate about the pleasure that lasts just a little bit. The devil says, "Guys, get excited about a game but not about God. Plan your next vacation, but don't plan your next devotion. Put bread on the table, but don't provide food for her soul. If the enemy can get a guy amped up about a football game or a video game or a promotion or a vacation or his car or his yard or anything besides God, a husband leads his wife into sin and sadness. He becomes the family drug dealer, giving his home hits of happiness but robbing them of sobriety, of being satisfied with God.

Guys, what your wife wants is God. Flowers are fine,

but God never wilts. His grace never falls like dead petals on the kitchen table. Marble countertops are great, but only God is the Rock who can support her soul through stress and kids and cancer. Vacations are fun, but only Jesus can give rest to her soul, a rest she doesn't have to work for, pay for, a rest that never ends. Deep in her heart is a longing to be loved, and God will always love her. There's a longing to be beautiful, and God will smile even at her wrinkling face. She has a longing to do something that matters, and God promises every cup of water she gives to the kids in Jesus' name will not be forgotten. Men are temporary people who can give temporary gifts. But by God's grace, a husband can lead his wife to the eternal God. That's how she'll live happily ever after.

That's what Drew knew. Drew Holcomb is the husband of Christian singer Ellie Holcomb. When Ellie tells the story of Drew's marriage proposal, the script isn't what you'd expect: an elaborate setup, promises to put her first and treat her like a princess forever. No, Drew said something like this: "I'm going to fail you. But God won't. So I want to lead you to God." That's a happy wife. That's a happy life.

That's the blueprint for husbands, but what about wives? What is their call in marriage? Look back at Genesis chapter 2:

The Lord God said, "It is not good for the man to be alone. I will make a helper suitable for him."

Now the L*ORD* God had formed out of the ground
all the wild animals and all the birds in the sky.
He brought them to the man to see what he
would name them; and whatever the man called
each living creature, that was its name. So the
man gave names to all the livestock, the birds in
the sky and all the wild animals.

But for Adam no suitable helper was found.
(verses 18-20)

Ladies, don't be offended by the title. *Helper* in Hebrew
is the word *ezer*, and it is almost always used to describe
God. Like the name Eleazar. Literally "El" or "God" is my
"ezer," my helper. The name implies that you have the
strength to give the help someone else needs.

But what help did Eve's husband need? Why weren't
the animals suitable helpers? Monkeys could climb trees
and pick fruit. Dogs could dig holes and bury seeds. But
what the zoo couldn't do was seek God. Only Adam had
a soul. So he needed a soulmate. That's why God made
woman. Her call would be simple: to help God's plan to
satisfy her man.

Wives, what your husbands need are not home-
cooked meals or new trucks or more sex. What they need
is God. That's the only thing that will satisfy their souls.
And husbands forget how to be happy so quickly. They
get tricked into thinking if only they had more (fill in the

blank). And they waste their lives pursuing what won't satisfy. But you can help them. Help them see the glory and power and plan of God. Help them see their purpose, no matter their job. Help them see their worth, no matter their net worth. Help them see their riches in heaven. Pray for them. Text a passage to them. Post a promise of God on the bathroom mirror. Help them remember that everything is temporary but God's mercy endures forever.

And help them remember God is with them. Have you ever heard of how Martin Luther's wife, Katie, helped him get back to God? Luther was moping and pouting because of the stress he was under until one day Katie came downstairs dressed completely in black.

"Why the dress?" Martin asked.

"A funeral," Katie replied.

"Who died?" Martin asked.

"Based on how you're acting, I assumed God did."

Boom! That's kind of snarky but kind of awesome. She was helping her husband remember God. God is bigger than this sin, stronger than this struggle. Jesus died for that. "Honey, you are holy! (My holy hubby!) And our God is good." Whenever a wife gets her guy back to God, that's the blueprint, because a wife is called to help God's plan to satisfy her man.

Look how the chapter ends:

So the Lord God caused the man to fall into a deep sleep; and while he was sleeping, he took one

of the man's ribs and then closed up the place with flesh. Then the Lord God made a woman from the rib he had taken out of the man, and he brought her to the man.

The man said,

"This is now bone of my bones and flesh of my flesh; she shall be called 'woman,' for she was taken out of man."

That is why a man leaves his father and mother and is united to his wife, and they become one flesh.

Adam and his wife were both naked, and they felt no shame. (verses 21-25)

God made a woman from a rib, which is weird, but maybe it's a beautiful picture that a husband is supposed to protect his wife's heart by leading her to God? Then God made marriage. He brought Eve to Adam. They became one flesh,

The point of marriage is the pursuit of God.

one family with one focus—to find happiness in God. I'd summarize the blueprint this way: the point of marriage is the pursuit of God. That's how a husband leads. That's how a wife helps. That's the blueprint.

But I can't leave you with just a blueprint. You need more than that. You need a blessing, and it's a phrase that's repeated eight times in this chapter's reading. Eight times! Did you catch it? **"Now the** LORD **God had planted . . . the** LORD **God made . . . the** LORD **God took . . . the** LORD **God commanded . . . the** LORD **God said . . . the** LORD **God had formed . . . the** LORD **God caused . . . the** LORD **God made a woman . . . and brought her to the man."** All over this blueprint is the LORD God.

I adore that! God in Hebrew is the word *Elohim*. It implies power and majesty and strength. Whenever you see God, think "great." The word LORD (all capitals) is the Hebrew *Yahweh*. It implies God's faithfulness, his love, his constant presence. When you see LORD, think "love." Put the two together, the LORD God, and you have power and love.

Which sounds a lot like Jesus. Like the perfect husband, Jesus gave up everything to lead his beloved back to God. Sin brought death, separated us from God, cursed us with sadness, but Jesus died to deal with our sin. He ate the fruit from the tree of death, the cross, so that we could eat from the tree of life and live with God forever. Jesus showed his love when he contained his power and bled red so we could be washed and dressed in white, like a bride on her wedding day. And like the perfect wife, Jesus helped. He sent the Holy Spirit to open our eyes to know God, to find joy in God, to picture the presence of God, to satisfy our souls.

That Jesus, that God, is with us to forgive us when we fail, to empower us when we're weak. The Prince who pursued his love. The One who promised to rescue us, to bring us back into the presence of God, so we could live happily ever after.

Study Questions

1. Why do people choose to get married? What are the dangers of getting married for reasons other than the reason God teaches us in Genesis chapter 2?

2. Read Proverbs 31:10-31 (especially verse 30). How do these famous words support this chapter's message?

Marriage Truths for Men and Women

Home is where the heart is, where a heart is either helped or hurt. As a pastor, most of my lowest lows and my highest highs happen because of my congregation members' homes, their relationships, their marriages. I looked through the names of my church family, searching for those who've been affected by divorce or struggling marriages. I thought of the adults who have reached out for help and the affected kids in their families. I thought of all those conversations in my office, the brokenness, the tears, the hurt. Sin always hurts, but when it happens in a home, it hurts a lot. But I noticed something else at my church. Happy homes. Couples I had seen downtown holding hands on dates. Marriages that weren't getting stale but getting better as the years went by. Kids who were growing up with a mom and a dad who loved, even liked, each other. And I realized how much it matters when men and women get this right at home. When they get marriages right, it helps so much. It honors God so much.

That's why we all care about our homes, whether we are personally married or single or divorced. Because I bet you want what I want and what God wants, for the homes of your best friends and closest family and church family to thrive as our Father intends, to be blessed by his design. You want to know it, embrace it, encourage it, live it. If so, Jesus' friend Peter is ready to help. In one of his letters to first-century Christians, Peter spoke to husbands and wives about God's design for our homes. We got some of the blueprint in Genesis, but God had more to say through Peter.

Let's start with the husbands. Here's what Peter says: **"Husbands, in the same way be considerate as you live with your wives"** (1 Peter 3:7). Guys, be thoughtful. Be attentive. Women are not mass produced in a female factory. They are uniquely and wonderfully made. So be considerate. Consider the woman you're with. Consider her personality (does she like to talk? be vulnerable? share the feelings behind the facts of your day?). Consider her interests (will watching the game or taking a walk or having sex help her connect?). Consider her past (how have men treated her, and can you imitate the good ones and distance your behavior from the bad ones?). Just consider her! Every woman knows intimacy is "into-me-see." See into me, into my heart, and consider me.

Which is why I have some homework if you are a husband. First, I want you to make a Considerate List, a list of things you've considered about her, learned about her. Second, I want you to share the list, ask if you missed anything important, and take notes on her answers. Finally, I want you to prepare to be kissed. I'm predicting a 57% success rate on that. Because you will become a rib that makes her feel safe, appreciated, and loved.

Truth #2 from Peter: **"And treat them with respect as the weaker partner"** (verse 7). Don't be offended, ladies. Peter is not a chauvinist. He's just repeating what we learned in the beginning. That God made men and women physically unique. In skeletal muscle and average size, men are stronger and women are weaker. Two separate women I interviewed mentioned this to me. When I go out for a run, I never worry about getting harassed or attacked, not even in Chicago or Israel. But women have to think about such things. Not because men are more sinful but because sinful men can misuse their strength and abuse the weaker partner. And Peter doesn't want husbands to do that.

Guys, let me be blunt with you. If you're doing that at home, be a man and get help. I don't care how stressful things are at work or how many beers you had in you that night. If the size of your body or the strength of your personality is scaring her, be a man and get help. God has called men to be like ribs and protect the people in their lives. Let's make sure they feel protected.

Truth #3 from Peter in verse 7: **"And treat them with respect as the weaker partner and as heirs with you of**

the gracious gift of life, so that nothing will hinder your prayers." That statement is stunning. Ladies, you are heirs too. In an age where women were so often diminished and dismissed, Peter said that they were heirs with their husbands. They would one day inherit the gracious gift of life, eternal life, life with God. The front-row seats around Jesus' throne wouldn't be gender specific but rather men and women, heirs together. And, guys, don't miss this—Christian women are heirs *with you*. Despite your sins, Jesus hasn't disinherited you. Men get the gift too. Men get the grace too. Men too are alive, spiritually connected to God because of the death and resurrection of Jesus. How great is that!

Guys, this is why the most important thing you will ever do, for yourselves and for your relationships, is to run to Jesus, to grab the hand of whoever is in your home and lead them to Jesus. The best way to be a man at home, to be a rib that protects your family, is by leading them to Jesus. The best way to be the "head of your household" is to listen and see your family's struggles and speak to them about Jesus. This is your call, the most important thing you will ever do, your privilege as sons of God.

Husbands, there's Peter's crash course on a holy home. Be considerate. Use your strength with respect. Treat her as a fellow heir of eternal life. And all the women said, "Amen! Let it be so with our husbands in our homes."

Now it's the ladies' turn. Peter has three truths for

you too. **"Wives, in the same way submit yourselves to your own husbands so that, if any of them do not believe the word, they may be won over without words by the behavior of their wives, when they see the purity and reverence of your lives"** (1 Peter 3:1,2). Ladies, God wants you to submit. In fact, it's apparently so important that he says it here and in Ephesians chapter 5 and in Colossians chapter 3. It's the essential calling of a wife. But what does it mean?

Here's what it *doesn't* mean. It doesn't mean you're an inferior, mousy doormat under your man's feet. Jesus submitted to his Father, and he wasn't anybody's doormat. He was the strong Son of God. And submission doesn't mean to stay in a dangerous situation. Sometimes leaving or calling the cops is the best way to help a broken man get better. No, here's what *submit* means: To put him first. To respect him. To honor him with your words and actions. To help him embrace the unique calling God has given him. Notice how powerful that

Here's what *submit* means: To put him first. To respect him.

is. It can actually change the hearts of unbelieving husbands. Selfless, respectful, you-first people are so rare. That behavior can actually bring a man to God!

Ladies, this calling will be crazy hard. In fact, one female author I read called this female porn. She was devastated when she discovered her husband's purity problem and furious when she found out how many

Christian men struggled with that sin. But it forced her to wrestle with the questions—Are men just worse than women? Are they the only ones who deeply wound their spouses with their choices? That didn't seem right. So after much thought and prayer and dialogue with God, she offered a controversial thought—What if disrespect was the female version of porn? What if the thousand tiny cuts of criticism—correcting his work, interrupting him to tell the "right" version of stories, treating him like one of the children, assuming your way is the right way, ignoring his

Our Father knows best. attraction to you—what if that hurt him as badly as a sordid search history did you? And what if it seemed as normal as a wandering eye is for a guy? When I first read that book, it seemed a bit out there. But then I started to see it everywhere. And I'd watch how guys would react to it. The embarrassment. The silence. The distance.

Our Father knows best. And he knows that a man craves respect. A man thrives when he is honored by willing submission. He stands up like a rib and protects his family if they have treated him like the church treats Jesus. So Peter says, "Wives, submit to your husbands."

That's the first truth. Ladies, here's truth #2: **"Your beauty should not come from outward adornment, such as elaborate hairstyles and the wearing of gold jewelry or fine clothes. Rather, it should be that of your inner self, the unfading beauty of a gentle and quiet spirit, which is of great worth in God's sight"** (verses 3,4).

Most women have a deep longing for beauty—for the skin, the hair, the shoes, the look. This is why you use the word *cute* a billion times more than your brothers! Beauty is great, but Peter knows it doesn't last. Outward beauty fades. No college guys try to pick up girls at the nursing home. So seek unfading beauty, the kind of spiritual life that is of great worth to God.

We are so blessed at my church to have so many women like that. The women who seek God Sunday after Sunday. The women who join our small groups and whose names I see growing on the Bible App. The women who pray every day and talk to their kids about Jesus. They are so wise. Because as their bodies grow older and weaker, their beauty gets better and stronger. That is of great worth in God's sight. Or as that famous Proverb about the noble woman puts it: **"Charm is deceptive, and beauty is fleeting; but a woman who fears the Lord is to be praised"** (31:30).

Which brings us to truth #3: **"For this is the way the holy women of the past who put their hope in God used to adorn themselves"** (1 Peter 3:5). The holy women, the women who were set apart from culture, who were wonderfully different, used to submit to their husbands. And don't miss this—they put their hope in God.

Your hope is your for-sure future. It's what God guarantees will happen one day. And holy women put their hope in God. They know they are heirs of eternal life and that Jesus died and rose so they would be for ever and ever loved and cherished and beautiful and blessed. No matter what happens in their homes, they know what happens in heaven. They get to be with Jesus, the perfect groom to his bride, the unfailing source of love and life, the Savior who will protect them forever. They get to serve with no strings attached, wanting but not needing their husbands to respond with love because they know they are pleasing the Jesus who gives them peace, the Jesus who loves no matter what, the Jesus who is their strength, their joy, their hope.

So put it all together and you have a home that can bless the heart. Husbands, be considerate, treat them with respect, remember they are heirs together with you. Wives, submit, seek lasting beauty, and put your hope in God. The more we can do that, with God's help, the more men will protect their wives and the more wives will help their husbands. The stronger our homes, our churches, and our faith will be.

A while back I woke up to an email in my inbox. It was from a woman who has two homes, a broken one with her ex and a happy one with her husband. She had been studying this passage from Peter and felt com-pelled to write me these words: "Having been divorced and remarried, I can tell you that THIS is absolutely the recipe for a great, God-pleasing marriage and, there-fore, a happy one." Then she told me about her current husband. No, she showed me about her husband. A text thread of his actual words. He considered her, respected her, but best of all, he texted, "I love you more, but Jesus loves you the most."

That is my prayer for every home, for your home. I pray that there would be love, 1 Peter kind of love, but that you would always know that Jesus loves you the most.

Study Questions

1. Compare this chapter's verses from 1 Peter with Ephesians 5:21-33 and Colossians 3:18,19. What similarities do you see? What additional points does Paul make in those sections?

2. Evaluate: Once a husband or wife makes their love conditional (i.e., "I will put you first only if you put me first"), a marriage will spiral toward divorce.

What Makes Marriage Work (and Wonderful)

In the last chapter, we looked at the marriage truths God gave to husbands and wives through the apostle Peter. But our LORD God has more to say to those who are married or will be married. What should you do (or not do) to have a happy, holy home?

Let's start with the guys again. I recently typed "husbands" and "married" and "marriage" into a Bible search engine, and what I discovered was golden. This passage seems like a helpful summary: **"A married man is concerned about the affairs of this world—how he can please his wife"** (1 Corinthians 7:33). A married Christian man is not just concerned about Christ in heaven but also about his wife on earth. Specifically—don't miss this phrase—how he can "please his wife." What is pleasing to her? What puts a smile on her face? A holy husband cares about that. To use the apostle Paul's language in this verse, a holy husband is "concerned" about that. His passion is pleasing his wife.

Then in the "husband" passages that I searched, I found seven specific commands, what I'm calling 7 Commandments for Husbands. Write these down or highlight them right in this book: Be considerate. Don't be harsh. Treat with respect. Love. Love. Love. Love. Ha! Dudes must depend on repetition! Love her, do what makes her feel loved, consider what's loving in her eyes, respect the way she receives love. That's your holy work that will help create a happy home.

Here's the most famous example: **"Husbands, love your wives, just as Christ loved the church and gave himself up for her"** (Ephesians 5:25). Just like Jesus, love will cost you. If she's wired differently than you, your love will have to be intentional, and if she wants differently than you, your love will likely be inconvenient. But this is how you can please your wife—love, love, love, love her.

Guys, do I have your attention? What I am about to write is a gender stereotype, but it is very often true. It is, I believe, what married women want. My friend told me that a man should never claim to know what women want, but I'm going to take a chance here (and you ladies can tell me if I'm way off).

[Special update—The paragraph that follows is the first piece of viral content that I have ever produced. It was viewed more than 1,000,000 times in less than three weeks on Instagram alone and shared tens of thousands of times. Apparently,

couples found this advice to be true and essential to marital happiness. Ready for it?]

The best husbands act without being asked. Guys, let me write that again so you don't miss it. The best husbands act without being asked. Most modern women do more things and carry more stress than we realize. They go to work, work hard, and then come home to hard work—the house, the cooking, the cleaning, the emails, the schedules. (If you have kids, multiply the weight of that last sentence by 17!) Thus, few things mean more than when a husband who loves his wife sees her stress and tries to solve it without being asked. If she asks for help and you give it, you are a good husband. If she doesn't even have to ask and it gets done, you are a great one.

But you might object: "I can't read her mind! I can't somehow know without being told!" Maybe not. Or maybe so. Husbands, think of marriage like fantasy football. If you've ever had a fantasy team, you (1) examine the data you have in order to (2) make this week the best it can be. You listen to a podcast or check a website to find out who is playing whom, who is injured, who is playing well, and who is not. You use that information to make specific decisions that give you the greatest chance of success.

What if you did that with marriage? What if you simply (1) examined the data you have to (2) make this week the best it can be? Ask her about her week, listen to her answers, note what stresses her, peek at her to-do list, and then act! Without being asked, react to her emotions. I guarantee that she will be stunned. And grateful. And find you very, very, very attractive.

If you're a guy, God has called you to be the head of your household, to be the first to love like Jesus, so act without being asked. That's what leads you to a happy, holy home.

In 2021 archaeologists in northern China discovered a couple like that. Inside of an ancient grave, 1,500 years old, they found two skeletons, not side by side but with arms wrapped around each other. The archaeologists, upon examining the remains, suggested that this couple had found "eternal love." I like that. You want something eternal, don't you? Love that lasts. Not five years and then fizzled out. That's why God is helping you here with a clear and direct call to action. Don't wait until you feel respected; just do what makes her feel loved. Be devoted to pleasing your wife, and you'll lead the way to a happy, holy home.

Alright, ladies, your turn. What does your Father in heaven say to you about your marriage here on earth? Kind of the same thing: **"A married woman is concerned about the affairs of this world—how she can please her husband"** (1 Corinthians 7:34). Every wife must constantly ask herself, "What pleases my husband? What's pleasing to my husband?" Ladies, if that question never slips down your list of priorities, if you never push pause on that question because of your job or your kids or your screens, you will be blessed. If, to steal Paul's word again, your "concern" is to that question—How can I please my husband?—your home is highly likely to be very happy and very holy.

Then, when I studied those same passages on marriage, I discovered the 7 Commandments for Wives. God, in his Word, commands seven specific things to his beloved daughters. Write these down or highlight them: Respect. Love. Be subject to. Submit. Submit. Submit. Submit. Interesting. And perhaps a bit uncomfortable.

Before you check out on me, let's remember that this is God's list. This isn't the Patriarchy Club saying, "Yeah. Let's put *submit* down four times just to keep them in their place!" No, this is God speaking. This is the God of love whom you pray to, the Jesus who saved you, and the Lord whom you trust.

Second, let's remember what *submit* means. It's what Jesus did when he put the Father first and said, **"Not as I will, but as you will"** (Matthew 26:39). Submitting doesn't mean you're inferior or unintelligent any more than Jesus was inferior or unintelligent. It simply means that when there's a difference, you put him first. When you can't do it your way and his way, you humbly submit to his way instead of forcing him to submit to your way. At the heart of submission is a you-first heart.

At the heart of submission is a you-first heart.

Ladies, this is a stereotype that isn't always true but one I hear all the time from men in struggling marriages.

I'll try to summarize it. Ready? Here goes—sex.

I know that's a stereotype, and I know that sex can be complicated for many reasons, but statistically 75% of husbands have a higher desire for intimacy than their wives. You might not be as interested as often, and that's okay, but that difference is your chance to show him love. When you care as much about this as you do your kids' education, your career, or your favorite show, that makes a man feel so respected. When you respond to his advances, he feels like a man. When you initiate the advances, he feels like *the* man. Honestly, most guys I know would rather wear dirty clothes and eat ramen seven days in a row if their wives were passionate about passion (and all the married men said, "Amen!").

Set this book down and put your fingers up (hold up two index fingers a few inches apart). Every day spouses

Love, submit, love, submit.

make choices that either draw them closer or push them apart. Be considerate about her needs (move closer). Respect his wants (move closer). Care more about work (move away). Give all your energy to the kids (move away). Love, submit, love, submit, love, submit, love, submit (move closer and closer and closer). There is someone in this world, in real life or online, who will notice her, listen to her, compliment her. Let it be you. There is someone who will respect him, flirt with him, make him feel like a man. Let it be you. Let it be you who vowed, "I will." God knows that selfless love, you-first submission that imitates Jesus is what makes a happy, holy home.

No wonder Paul started with Jesus. Most of the passages I shared with you in this chapter come from the writings of the apostle Paul, and they have something in common—they come later in his letters. All those "husbands, love" and "wives, submit" commands come in the middle, if not the very end, of what Paul wrote to various churches. Want to guess what Paul always said first? Jesus.

Before 1 Corinthians chapter 7 said to **"be concerned"** about your spouse, 1 Corinthians chapter 1 said, **"Christ Jesus . . . is our righteousness, holiness and redemption"** (verse 30). Because Jesus loved, loved, loved, loved you, you are right with God. You are holy in his sight, even if you've done some unholy things in your relationship. You are redeemed, bought with the price that he paid at the cross.

Before Colossians chapter 3 said, **"Submit . . . love,"** Colossians chapter 1 said, **"**[God] **has reconciled you by Christ's physical body through death to present you holy in his sight, without blemish and free from accusation"** (verse 22). Because Jesus submitted, submitted, submitted, submitted to his Father, you are reconciled to the Father, completely one with God. You are holy in his sight, forgiven for everything you've done wrong in life and in love, with no sin left to make God accuse you. Before Ephesians chapter 5 said, **"Submit . . . love,"** Ephesians chapter 1 said, **"Praise be to the God and Father of our Lord Jesus Christ, who has blessed** us in the heavenly realms with every spiritual blessing in Christ" (verse 3). Every spiritual blessing! If you have Jesus, you are forgiven and loved and saved and guarded and kept and chosen and precious and invited and included and accepted and bound for the most blessed life with God.

Do you see? Marriage starts with Jesus. It always starts with Jesus. What makes us so happy and completely holy is Jesus, who, like a perfect husband, loved us by giving up everything and, who like a perfect wife, submitted to

Marriage starts with Jesus.

the plan the Father had to save us. That love is so foundational, so transformational, that when we get married, there is only one way to live—like Jesus. Husbands, love like Jesus. Wives, submit like Jesus. It isn't easy. But it is the path to a happy, holy home.

My friend gets that. Remember my buddy from this book's introduction and his 50-year anniversary party? When I emailed him about the party, I also asked him to give me some details about marriage in his family. He responded with a section that contained 310 words (I counted). And guess how many of those words were about Jesus? (I also counted.) Let me quote some of what he wrote: *"Blessings, blessing, God, grace, forgiveness, prayer, Lord, bless, God, pray, pray, Lord, grace, faith, bless, God, God, forgiving, grace, blessings, forgiveness, prayers, prayers, Savior, Lord, blessed, blessings, blessed, Jesus, Jesus, God bless."* Out of 310 words, 32 were about Jesus! In the midst of all the differences and disagreements, all the sin and stress, was Jesus. I'll let my friend have the last word: *"Both my wife and I had parents who were blessed with over 60 years. We both remember talking with our parents about how foolish it is for people to think that there would never be rough spots or bumpy roads. We are all sinners. We need Jesus, and we all have Jesus."*

We all need Jesus. Through faith, we all can have Jesus. No matter how many people live under your roof, Jesus is the heart of a happy and holy home.

Study Questions

1. Whether you are single, married, dating, or divorced, take ten minutes today to pray for the married couples that you know. Ask our Father to guide them to put this chapter into practice.

2. Study Ephesians 5:22-33, one of the longest sections in the Bible about marriage. Which words/phrases grab your attention? Why?

3. Agree/Disagree: "Do without being asked" is a way for couples to divorce-proof their marriage.

Adultery:
How to Avoid It and
What to Do After It

We've spent some time talking about what makes a happy, holy home. But what happens when the unthinkable happens? What about when your spouse cheats? A while back, my church family, sadly, had a series of unfaithful marriages. As I tried to help this couple and that couple and this other couple, three things struck me—them and me and you.

Them—They were not once-in-a-while church people whom I barely knew but every-Sunday, Bible-reading, deeply rooted Christians. And yet adultery happened to them, and when it did, they struggled to know what to do, even how to function.

Me—And I, despite all my knowledge of the Bible, didn't know exactly how to help. Since I had never experienced it, I didn't really get it. The things some people said confused me. The way some people felt didn't make sense to me. My advice too often seemed shallow and unrealistic.

You—People like you were affected too. Friends were pulled into complex relational dynamics that challenged their friendships. They took a step away, not knowing quite what to do. Others got overly involved. They didn't have a script to follow, which explained the confusion and frustration.

After thinking about them and me and you, I realized that I needed to address another tough topic—adultery.

Few things are as common and as catastrophic and as complex as adultery. In a culture where 1 out of 5 husbands and 1 out of 8 wives will be unfaithful, adultery, sooner or later, will be part of your life or your loved ones' lives. Maybe that's you right now. Maybe you two are on this ultramarathon of rebuilding trust and moving past the pain and finally feeling the tiniest bit of hope. Or maybe you are still stuck in the shame and the pain, and you don't know how to move on or forgive or feel what you used to feel. You're on autopilot. You're numb. You're just trying to survive. Or maybe you haven't cheated but, honestly, you're close. Things are stale at home, you don't feel like his priority, but there's that guy from work or that girl online who has your attention and your attraction. Or maybe you love someone whose love has been rocked by a broken vow. Your friend just came clean. Your sister admitted an affair. And now you're trying to figure out what to do and what to say and how to help, and people are picking sides, blaming, suggesting, gossiping, giving up. It's a mess, and you don't know how to help them heal.

All that is why I need to address this. For the next two chapters, let's talk about something I wish I didn't have to talk about—adultery. Let's open the Bible and see what God has to say to help us and help us help them. We won't be able to cover everything, but in this chapter I want to share five biblical truths about adultery.

Ready for truth #1? *Don't!* When it comes to adultery, God says, "Don't!" In fact, of the 55 uses of the word *adultery* in the Bible, the very first one that shows up is this: **"You shall not commit adultery"** (Exodus 20:14). You shall not. Why not? Because adultery butchers God's blessings. It takes the "one flesh" of marriage and rips it in two. Committing adultery, as one author says, is like hosting a picnic with the people you love on an interstate. Eventually, your sin will smash into your life like a cement truck, and the carnage will be your fault.

Have you ever considered the consequences of adultery? Like the loss of trust. The half-truths and the total lies will take away one of marriage's most underappreciated gifts—trust. If you cheat, he won't trust you to look at your phone, to go out with friends, to travel for work, to be on the computer, to come home late, to run a quick errand after work. Every hour of every day, she will wonder where you are and with whom you are and what you might be doing.

And then there are the triggers. Everything connected with the affair will trigger her. The device you used to DM her. The job where you worked with her. The date you confessed to her. The church where you worshiped with her. People, places, and things will now be traumatizing for her in a way you never thought about, because you were not thinking about her. You should fear adultery more than you fear fentanyl. The Bible says that road leads to death. It's like starting a campfire in your lap. It can ruin you, and you must run from it.

In 1941 a woman from the Soviet Union was put in a Nazi concentration camp where she witnessed murders, lost family members, and endured Hitler's horrors. But she survived, got married, and, sadly, was cheated on. And this Holocaust survivor said, "The affair was the most painful experience of my life."[5] More painful than Hitler was what that man did to her. Don't.

That's how affairs happen. We get too close.

Truth #2—*Don't come close!*

Picture it this way: Imagine me standing at the edge of a stage. On the stage is a faithful marriage, and down below the stage is an affair. Few people, if any, think they would ever cheat, but what happens is that they get close and then they slip. That's how affairs happen. We get too close.

Every act of adultery is unique, but there is a fairly predictable pattern. Highlight this: It starts with deprivation. When one spouse feels deprived of attention or affection or someone who will listen, they can get desperate. Desperate for someone who notices them, who compliments them, who flirts with them, who initiates physical touch with them, who makes them feel like they matter. Step 2—Attraction. You notice her. You start to think of him. She's your type. He gives you the butterflies. It could be her looks or his personality, but you feel something different with them. Step 3—Intention. You do something with the intention of connection with the person of your attraction. You go out of your way to stop by her office. You do your hair for the Zoom call because he's going to be in that little square. Step 4—Emotion. You open up about emotional stuff, about hurts and hopes and dreams, and—don't miss this—about your struggles with your spouse when you're not with your spouse. When your confidant is your crush, you are so close. In fact, if your biggest emotional connection is with them, you are already having an emotional affair. Step 5—Connection. A physical connection. Once you touch someone who has touched your heart, your toes are over the edge. One author admitted, *"I offered [her] a friendly shoulder. That offer of comfort became much more within seconds. Falling was much easier than I'd ever believed possible."*[6] Those are the steps that lead you over the edge.

Maybe you see yourself in one of these steps, but you never would step over the edge. Listen! No one thinks they will. So before you fall, take a step back. Even if it's awkward. Even if she's confused by your behavior. Even if your friends think you're being a prude. Some people call these guardrails, personal habits that keep us from getting too close to a catastrophic fall. It's why I will never meet privately with a woman at church if no one is around. It's why some women won't text a married friend unless his wife is on the thread. It's why others share their passwords with their spouses, so there are no places for secrets. It's why the smartest spouses ask each other often, "How are we doing? How can I love you better?" There's little room for deprivation when you're that devoted to your marriage.

If you think this is all a bit dramatic, listen to what Jesus said about it. In his famous teaching on adultery and lust, he said, **"If your right eye causes you to stumble, gouge it out and throw it away. It is better for you to lose one part of your body than for your whole body to be thrown into hell"** (Matthew 5:29). The point? It's better to take a drastic step than end up with a devastating ending.

Which brings us to truth #3, perhaps the most essential thing I have learned from all my studies. Highlight this: *Healing = Time x Work x Work.* Couples who commit adultery can heal. They can. They have. They will. Some, by the pure grace of Jesus, end up with stronger marriages than they had before. You might not believe that yet, but it is true. God can heal your marriage. And here's how God heals marriages—Time, Work, and Work.

First, time. You know the saying, right? Time heals . . .

all wounds. This wound is a big one. Adultery is like a bus hitting a pedestrian, and there is no shortcut to getting back on your feet by Friday. You can work, she can work, work with a counselor, work with a pastor, work on yourselves, work together, but if time equals almost 0, your healing will be minimal. It takes time.

How much time? Since every couple is different, I'm reluctant to suggest an answer, but many authors say about two years. Two years after the last secret is out is when many couples mutually feel like they're going to make it. Because you need time to talk about everything and then time to talk about everything again and then time to talk about everything again and again. Time for him to play detective, to ask every question, for her to "have an affair with the affair," obsessing over everything. I wish it was faster, but it isn't. Healing takes time.

And work. The one who cheated must work. Two years can pass, but if you multiply 2 x 0, the healing is 0. I won't lie to you. If you stepped over that edge, you have so much work to do. In four thousand different ways, you will have to be humble. Like telling the whole truth. You cannot— please hear me!—you cannot trickle out the truth. I know you're scared the whole story will make them leave you, but you cannot, must not, please do not lie to them again. Do the necessary work of telling them the truth. And then the real work begins. You will have to talk when he wants to talk. You will have to give her the right to your phone whenever she wants. You will have to accept her absolute disgust with sex for the time being. You will have to resist the temptation to yell, "I already answered that question!" No, instead, you must do the holy work of humility. You-first is always important in marriage but never more important than after an affair. If that's you, then make "work" the biggest number it can be. Because Healing = Time x Work . . .

. . . x Work. This is probably the hardest thing I'm going to write here, but if Healing = Time x Work x Work, then the one cheated on must work too. If you don't work, this won't work.

Years ago, I tried patiently to help a couple heal from a devastating affair. Lots of time had passed, and the husband, who had cheated, had done so much work. One day I asked his wife, "What are you doing to serve him these days?" And she said, "Letting him live in our house." I smiled. She smiled. We laughed. Then she said, "That sounds bad, doesn't it?" (She said I could share that story with you.)

I get it. No, I don't get it here (heart), but I get it here (head). You are the one who was betrayed. You are the one who can't sleep. You are the one whose life got turned upside down. That's true. The Bible doesn't command you to stay after an affair, but if you do stay, then you still have a vow to keep and you don't get a free pass to sin. There is good work for you to do on yourself. Because, even before this happened, you were a sinner. In fact, you were a sinful spouse. You had stuff to work on then. You still do now. A fellow pastor likes to ask couples these questions: Before the affair, were you happy? Were you two close? Did you feel emotionally connected? Did you feel loved? Did you feel respected? Was your marriage, your communication, your sex life a bigger priority than work or the kids or the screens? If not, what good and holy work might God be calling both of you to do today?

I know that this work, for both of you, feels overwhelming. So let's bring God into it. Would you pray a familiar prayer from a fresh angle? Pray the Lord's Prayer, but this time think of what it means for couples dealing with adultery. Ready? **"Our Father in heaven, hallowed be your name. Your kingdom come. Your will be done on earth as it is in heaven. Give us today our daily bread. Forgive us our sins, as we forgive those who sin against us. Lead us not into temptation, but deliver us from evil. For yours is the kingdom, the power, and the glory, now and forever. Amen."**

Truth #4 is quick, because it's what the next chapter is about—*Run to them*. You will need them. Friends. Family. A counselor. A pastor. A network of people who know you, love your marriage, and want to help you with the healing equation. Your mind will be a mess, and every lie will be so easy to believe. You'll need help. You'll grow impatient with the process or think that you have the right to sin now. You'll need help. And that's what Christian friends are for. This is complicated and messy, so we'll spend the next chapter on the details. But for now, believe Paul's words: **"Carry each other's burdens, and in this way you will fulfill the law of Christ"** (Galatians 6:2).

Truth #5—*Run to Him.* Run to God. Whether you cheated or were cheated on, run to God. If you cheated, here's what you need to know about God. He forgives people just like you. King David was just like you. He was married, and he was attracted to Bathsheba even though she was married. He had an affair and covered it up for an entire year. But when God sent the prophet Nathan to expose him, David repented, and God forgave him. Even for his adultery. David later sang, **"Then I acknowledged my sin to you and did not cover up my iniquity. I said, 'I will confess my transgressions to the Lord.' And you forgave the guilt of my sin"** (Psalm 32:5).

Whether you cheated or were cheated on, run to God.

That is true for you too. Confess to God. He will forgive the guilt. He will forgive the sin. That's what Jesus did. Before you crossed that line, our Lord knew it. Ever thought about that? Two thousand years ago, when Jesus was on a cross, he knew all about this. He knew her name. He knew your secret. And Jesus loved you so much— you!—that he took that massive weight on his shoulders and bore it on a cross. Jesus died for that. Jesus died for you. Jesus didn't just die for some sins. Jesus died for all sins so that no matter what happens to your marriage, you would know what happens with your God. Hear me, all you who have cheated. Because of Jesus, God likes you.

You might hate yourself, but God refuses to hate you. He won't. He never will.

And if you've been cheated on, run to God too. You might have wondered a million times what's wrong with you, why you're not good enough, why he chose her, why she didn't choose you. You might be appalled at all the bitterness and hate that are coming out of you. The best thing I can say is that God chooses you. Because of Jesus, you are always, today and forever, enough for God. He always has time for you. He is never tired of you. You can't run out of prayer minutes. You can't make Jesus sigh and roll his eyes. God is love. And he loves you. He chooses you today. And that choice, because of Christ, will never change. Your marriage may heal, or it may not. It may be better after the affair, or it may be worse. But at the end of every day, your relationship with God is perfect. Jesus made it that way. Nothing to fix. No trust to rebuild. No holding your breath. Jesus made it perfect. You have a spot in the happiest, holiest home of all, in heaven itself. And Jesus made sure that nothing will change that.

Friends, there is hope. It's what a local Christian counselor mentioned when I shared this chapter with him. "Things will be different, but they can be better than ever before." It's what a fellow pastor told me about his own experiences, about couples who committed to both do the work and wait on the Lord and ended up better than before. And it's what I heard from some couples I interviewed who had been there and made it to the other side, not just back to where they were but better than before. So I will leave you with one word—*hope*. Maybe not today, maybe not tomorrow, but you will be better than before. Work and wait until the Lord restores what sin has broken. He will do it, either in this life or the next. But if you have Jesus, you have hope. Believe that.

Study Questions

1. Which of the five truths impacted you the most while you read this chapter?

2. Read Galatians 6:1-10, finding at least three connections you see between Paul's words and the topic of infidelity.

3. Whom did you think of as you read this chapter? Share this message with them and pray that God would use it to give them hope.

Adultery:
When Friends Cheat

One of the hardest times to be a good friend is when your friend cheats (or is cheated on). When adultery happens by or to someone you love, it's hard to know what to do. What do you do when she is furious or numb or done, obsessed with what must be wrong with her, or unwilling to admit that anything is wrong with her? What do you say when he is so ashamed or not ashamed enough, when he is sick with guilt or when he's sick of talking about the same things over and over and over? What do you do when friends and family members are picking sides, pointing fingers, sharing gossip, or stepping back altogether? Statistically, sooner or later, adultery will happen in your family, your church, or among your friends. So what does being a Christian look like in those moments?

Here's a simple answer to that very complex question—when friends cheat, give them grace and truth. Give *them*. Both of them. Him and her. The betrayer and the betrayed. Grace and truth. *And.* Not one or the other but both. That's what you do. That's how you take God's side and help them rebuild, to the best of your ability, a happy, holy home. The gospel of John says that Jesus Christ was **"full of grace and truth"** (1:14). I want to help you be a little bit like Jesus and bring a whole lot of Jesus, which is what your friends need when your friends cheat.

I want to tell you up front that this chapter is a bit complicated, just like infidelity is complicated. I'm trying to squeeze into one chapter how you can help him and her with grace and truth. That's a lot of parts instead of one big idea, so you're going to need to take notes and try to take away something helpful, even if you can't recite every last thing you learn. Ready for that?

Let's start with the friend who was cheated on, the victim of adultery. What does it mean to show him or her grace? It means, maybe more than ever before, to show up and share Jesus. You don't need to be a professional, just be present. Be there for coffee. Be there when he needs to cry. Be there when she texts. Even if you don't have anything profound to share, be there. Proverbs 27:10 says, "Better a neighbor nearby than a relative far away." It's better to be closer. To just show up.

Sound easy? It's not. In the previous chapter, you learned that many experts suggest that it takes up to two years for unfaithful couples to start to heal. And that means that this will be a marathon that you are suddenly running without much training. That's the hard part. And because adultery isn't something couples share with the whole world, you might be only one of ten people or one of eight people or one of six people who knows. That's the harder part. And because adultery is adultery, that weight will weigh about a thousand pounds. That's the hardest part. This chapter of your friendship might feel pretty one-sided, like you're listening and listening and giving and giving and not getting a lot in return. Most friendships are fueled by fun experiences, but dealing with adultery isn't fun. Which is why most friends fade away.

But grace shows up. Not all the time. You're not God, and you're not a 24/7 counselor who has no life besides being a friend to this one friend. You are, however, called to be faithful. To shoulder that burden with them. So pray for the strength to be there. Commit yourself to giving more for the next year. "God, you put me here for such a time as this, to be here during his time of greatest need."

And while you're showing up, share Jesus. He's the best grace of all. When God's chosen ones get cheated on, they tend to think about the cheating and not on the choosing. So your calling is to give that person a rock to stand on. Remind her that

While you're showing up, share Jesus.

her identity, the deepest definition of who she is, isn't being the cute couple or the perfect family. No, her identity is as a child of God, and that hasn't changed. You get to bring this kind of grace to your hurting friend: that nothing will separate him from the love of God that is in

Christ Jesus (Romans 8:38,39). "You may feel separated from your spouse. But there is nothing in the world, not even this, that can separate you from Jesus' love." In her trauma, those words won't sink in, so keep saying them. "God chooses you. God is here with you. God loves you." Show up and share Jesus. That's grace.

Next, give him or her the truth. Here's a truth you may know that your friend needs to know. I wrote about this in the last chapter: Healing = Time x Work x Work. In the midst of the emotions, she'll forget that truth all the time, so encourage her, "You're doing the work. He's doing the work. You're talking. He's listening. You're going to counseling. It just takes time. I remember three months ago, you couldn't even smile, but I saw you smile today."

Or maybe he needs to hear some hard truth. I once asked a woman, "When you were trying to heal, did you need more of the gospel or the law? Did you need someone to remind you that you were loved, chosen, and beautiful to God? Or did you need someone to tell you, 'Stop sinning!'?" Her answer was immediate: the law. As she wrestled with vengeance, hatred, and pride, she needed her closest friends to say, "We love you, but you need to stop that." This same woman encouraged people to ask for permission. "If I ever see you sabotaging your own healing, can I say something?" That's good truth.

Picture grace/truth like a dumbbell. Ever done a shoulder raise? It's really hard to lift a lot of weight because the deltoid in the shoulder is relatively small, and this exercise isolates the muscle. In other words, the deltoid doesn't get a ton of help from the biceps or the pecs or the quads. Being cheated on is like doing deltoid raises with heavy weights. You can't. You can't do this alone. That's where friends show up. With grace and truth, we help them remember Jesus and do the work of Jesus. Grace and truth. That's how you help a friend who has been cheated on.

And—ready for the next part?—grace and truth are also how you help the one who cheated. What does grace look like in those conversations? Show up and share Jesus. Sound familiar? It is. Sound easy? It isn't. Adultery is so painful and so brutal that many people will keep their distance. "How can I be friends with you after what you did? If I hang out with you, people will think that I think what you did was okay. If you went after his wife, how do I know you won't go after mine?" Most people don't show up. But grace shows up.

Isn't that what Jesus did? **"Now the tax collectors and sinners were all gathering around to hear Jesus. But the Pharisees and the teachers of the law muttered, 'This man welcomes sinners and eats with them'"** (Luke 15:1,2). They muttered because Jesus showed up. He hated sin, but he loved sinners. And you can hate adultery but still love an adulterer. Put on your running shoes and jump into the marathon of healing by showing up.

And while you're showing up, share Jesus. I once

knew a married man who, unfortunately, crossed some emotional and physical lines with another woman. Fortunately, he was wrecked by his sin and repentant. He was sorry. But that sorrow made it hard for him to see the cross. His shame came in waves, especially as he realized all the consequences of his actions. So I made him a promise: "For the next month, I will text you a passage about God's grace every day. About forgiveness for all sin. For your sin." And I did, and he said it really helped. Could you do that too? You might not know the Bible like I do, but Google "best passages on forgiveness" and send them to your friend. Share Jesus. The grace of Jesus is what that friend needs.

And truth. Remember this? Tell your friend, "Healing = Time x Work x Work. It's your opportunity to do things a different way, to start over at square one, to talk about everything, to build your marriage on God's foundation. None of us would choose it, but God can use it. He can use this to help you prioritize each other, to communicate about everything, to listen without shutting down or blowing up. This is going to be harder than anything you've ever been through. This is going to make you humbler than anything you've ever been through. And this can make you holier and happier than you've ever been.

"But the truth is you'll have to work. One day at a time, God will call you to do good works. Like owning it. Own the wreckage. Accept that the consequences are your fault. He's obsessing, and you did that. She cries in the middle of making love, and you did that. A year later, he still wonders what you were doing during work, and you did that too. You have to own all that."

Say to your friend: "I know this sucks. But you reap what you sow, bro. So how can I help you get through this? Maybe the work is doing something nice, no matter what your spouse is doing for you. Put a note in her lunch with five things you respect about her. If she lets you, put your hand on her leg while she drives. Find a babysitter, take a walk, and agree to talk about something besides the affair, something good from your week, just for one hour. Go back to the basics—love and respect—think of your spouse and do it." As a friend, help him set a short-term goal and hold him to it. Applaud her if she makes it. She'll need the encouragement.

This passage summarizes that work so well: **"Do nothing out of selfish ambition or vain conceit. Rather, in humility value others above yourselves, not looking to your own interests but each of you to the interests of the others"** (Philippians 2:3,4). That's the work. You-first matters more than ever after adultery, and your friend will need encouragement to do it.

You-first matters more than ever after adultery.

That's what friends do. Grace and truth. Grace and truth. Grace and truth. That's how you choose God's side. That's how you help people heal.

So as I wrap up this discussion on adultery, I want

to end in an obvious way—banana bread. I love banana bread. Do you? Chocolate chip banana bread that is barely visible because of all the butter might be as close to heaven as you can get on this earth. My daughter Maya makes banana bread, and it rarely lasts 48 hours once the hungry vultures of our family descend upon it. But do you know the primary ingredient in banana bread? Bad bananas. Overripe, too smushy, too nasty to eat bananas are what ends up in banana bread. I don't quite know how that's possible, but it is true. And adultery is like that too. God takes something bad, something sinful, and he adds in time and work and work and friends who gave grace and truth to her and grace and truth to him. He covers the whole thing with Jesus, and, somehow, he brings out a blessing. A restored marriage. Or healing even if divorce happens. A family that makes it. Or friends who help friends make it through. We can't guarantee a happy ending for every family, but when friends show up full of grace and truth, there is always a blessing.

I'd like to end this with a blessing, one spoken by Jesus' own brother Jude. Whether you are healing or helping, may these words comfort you: **"Be merciful to those who doubt; save others by snatching them from the fire; to others show mercy, mixed with fear— hating even the clothing stained by corrupted flesh. To him who is able to keep you from stumbling and to present you before his glorious presence without fault and with great joy—to the only God our Savior be glory,** majesty, power and authority, through Jesus Christ our Lord, before all ages, now and forevermore! Amen" (Jude 1:22–24).

Study Questions

1. Close your eyes and try to remember the main points from this chapter. Can you recall them? Could you summarize them to a friend? If not, study your notes until God's truth is stored in your heart.

2. Proverbs 11:13 says, "A gossip betrays a confidence, but a trustworthy person keeps a secret." Why is being trustworthy a vital quality to helping friends after an affair?

3. Read Psalm 23. How might these words comfort a friend whose marriage didn't make it after adultery?

God's Crash Course on Divorce

A friend of mine once preached a sermon on divorce that lasted 49 minutes. I asked him what he would do differently if he would do it again. He answered immediately, "Preach longer." Despite the shock value, I understand why he said that. I've studied passages on divorce and interviewed people who've been divorced, and I have no clue how to say everything in under four hours. There are so many issues, so many deeply personal situations, so many questions, like . . .

Is divorce ever okay with God? What if you are profoundly unhappy? Or if the kids are hurting? Does God want you to live sadly ever after? Are there any good reasons to get a divorce? If she cheats? If he leaves? If she drinks? If he belittles? If she's emotionally abusive? If he's physically abusive? And why do the divorced so often feel second rate in churches? Like they don't exactly belong? Like everyone is watching, staring, judging? And what about heaven? Will Jesus forgive you if you get a divorce? Or does divorce equal damnation? And how do we help each other? What do you say if your son has already filed for divorce? If your sister wants to remarry after her divorce? What does God say about all this?

I couldn't answer all those questions in hours. But I do want to start this needed conversation with an open Bible. I want to open the Bible and answer four key questions about divorce—What does God think about divorce? What are godly reasons to divorce? What about life after divorce? What does God think about the divorced? I know what God says is always good and always for our good, so I pray that this chapter, which is admittedly shorter than it should be, brings you and those you love hope and healing.

Question 1:
What does God think about divorce?

In the beginning, God made marriage. He made a man, then a woman, and then a marriage. God brought her to the man, and the two became one. **"A man will . . . be united to his wife,"** Jesus said (Mark 10:7). In Greek, the verb literally means "glued" to her. Their relationship would be closer, more intimate, more vulnerable than any relationship on earth. **"Therefore what God has joined together, let no one separate"** (Mark 10:9).

Because if you try to separate two pieces of paper that

are glued together, there is no clean break, no simple separation. There are frayed edges, ripped-up hearts, divided children. There's the emotional exhaustion of custody battles and the kids who need two pillows for their two beds. There's the girl who wonders if her heavenly Father will leave her like her dad did. There's the man who flirts with an affair just to feel something again. There's the running away from your church, from your pastor, from your group, from your God. Divorce rips us apart when God wants us to be together.

That's not just what God says. It's what the divorced say. One man told me, "I hate divorce. I mean I hate it!! That feeling of absolute failure, rejection, and disappointment is awful." Another woman lamented, "How my kids have been affected. . . . It tears me up." Our Father hates divorce because he hates to see his beloved children suffer the consequences of one being torn into two.

Malachi 2:16 explains, **"'The man who hates and divorces his wife,' says the Lord, the God of Israel, 'does violence to the one he should protect.'"** God hates divorce because God hates hate. God hates it when a man doesn't love his wife, doesn't protect her like he should, doesn't serve her like Jesus served him. A husband's calling is to be like a rib, a strong, sacrificial servant who protects the "heart" of his marriage. When a man breaks that vow, he assaults the beauty of the institution God created. God hates that.

Divorce does not just happen. It is too traumatic for

anyone to wake up one day and choose it. Instead, divorce is the fruit of some other rotten root. Something is wrong beneath the surface, something has changed since the vows, something sinful started growing in a home, and what it produced was the desire for a divorce.

Maybe you idolized your needs—sex or romance or doing more around the house or whatever. You needed those needs, and you weren't going to serve or love unless those needs were met. You would work on her list only if and only after she worked on yours. Predictably,

Divorce is the fruit of some other rotten root.

your spouse turned around and did the same. And the crazy cycle of conditional love took root in your marriage.

Or maybe you idolized power. You wanted the promotion, the respect, the public image so much that you left your marriage on autopilot. You feared disappointing your boss more than disappointing your spouse. You would never interrupt work time for a phone call from your partner, but you told your family to be quiet while you took a work call at home. And the sad reality of being second place on your schedule took root in your spouse's heart.

Or maybe you idolized the kids. You filled the calendar with classes and lessons, and there was no time to love him, to flirt with him, to be with him. He's a grown man, right? He should understand that those 20 years of child raising won't be all that romantic, right?

Or maybe you idolized control. You had to get your

way. You had to win the argument. So you interrupted and raised your voice and brought up the past. After enough time, you gave up fighting, perhaps even gave up talking, which left your heart aching for something other than your own home.

That's why God hates divorce. God hates it when divorce happens because it proves something else happened first. The seed of sin took root and grew as the months moved by. And God, standing outside of time, viewing every divorce in human history at the same time, knows the damage. He hears the ripping apart, watches the bleeding, and weeps at the weeping of his sons and daughters. God hates divorce.

He has to. Because God loves marriage. Not just being married in general but being married biblically. Loving and serving, not because your spouse deserves it but because you follow the Lord of undeserved love. If God loves love itself, freely and sincerely given, how could he not hate divorce?

I got a fascinating phone call a few months ago from a former church member who is now formerly married (a.k.a. divorced). "Can you preach on divorce?" he asked me. I replied, "Can you tell me about yours?" He did. He told me about the toxic habit of keeping score. "In marriage," he said, "you divide up the household duties and then keep score. You expect your spouse to serve you because you served them." I am not shocked that such an attitude suffocated that marriage. Love keeps no record of their wrongs; neither does it keep a record of all my rights.

So what does God think about divorce? God hates it because he loves unconditional love.

Question 2:
What are godly reasons to divorce?

When Jesus was a kid, divorce was fiercely debated by two of the most famous rabbis of all time—Shammai and Hillel. Both of these spiritual leaders looked carefully at these words from the Torah: **"If a man marries a woman who becomes displeasing to him because he finds something indecent about her, and he writes her a certificate of divorce . . ."** (Deuteronomy 24:1). Then both men debated what Moses meant by "something indecent." Shammai said *indecent* meant "adultery." Hillel said it meant anything you didn't like, even the way she overcooked last night's dinner. They disagreed on decent reasons for divorce, circumstances that would allow God's faithful people to end a marriage.

In the middle of this debate, Jesus became a rabbi and got pulled into the debate:

Some Pharisees came to him to test him. They asked, "Is it lawful for a man to divorce his wife for any and every reason?"

"Haven't you read," he replied, "that at the beginning the Creator 'made them male and female,' and said, 'For this reason a man will leave his father and mother and be united to his wife, and the two will become one flesh'? So they are no longer two, but one flesh. Therefore what God has joined together, let no one separate."

"Why then," they asked, "did Moses command that a man give his wife a certificate of divorce and send her away?"

Jesus replied, "Moses permitted you to divorce your wives because your hearts were hard. But it was not this way from the beginning. I tell you that anyone who divorces his wife, except for sexual immorality, and marries another woman commits adultery." (Matthew 19:3-9)

Jesus took a side in this fierce and very personal theological debate. Except for "sexual immorality," you can't separate. You can't divorce. You can't remarry. Shammai was right. If you've been the victim of sexual immorality, you can get a divorce without sinning.

Or, better said, you can make public what your spouse has done in private. This is a point that people in the church too often miss, so please take note of what I am about to say. Filing for divorce does not mean the divorce is your fault. Did you hear that? Filing doesn't equal fault. The fault is in the sinner, the one who broke the marriage. God hates what first caused the marriage to end, not the first one to go to court to end the marriage. Sometimes the innocent feel guilty while the

The fault is in the sinner, the one who broke the marriage.

guilty claim innocence based on who filed the papers. I've known sexually immoral men who throw Malachi chapter 2 at their victimized wives who want a divorce. No, God walks with the innocent to court. So if your spouse cheated on you, making you the victim of sexual immorality, you and Jesus, if you choose, can go to court together and file for a divorce.

The apostle Paul adds a second reason for divorce. In his lengthy chapter on marriage and divorce, he writes:

A wife must not separate from her husband. But if she does, she must remain unmarried or else be reconciled to her husband. And a husband must not divorce his wife. But if the unbeliever leaves, let it be so. The brother or the sister is not bound in such circumstances; God has called us to live in peace. (1 Corinthians 7:10,11,15)

If he "leaves," you are not bound. You don't have to stay. You don't have to sit there for the next 60 years, rejected but with a ring on your finger. You can divorce.

God has called you to live in peace. This is often called the cause of desertion.

But notice something else. Paul says, "In such circumstances." Not, "In this circumstance," as if physically leaving were the only form of desertion. There are other circumstances when one person deserts the marriage. He might come home every night, but he has unilaterally, without cause, deserted his spouse.

Now let me tell you what this isn't. This isn't that common, crazy cycle where two spouses are stuck in a selfish standoff. You don't serve him because he doesn't serve you. She isn't going out of her way to love you, but you aren't putting in the effort to love her. That's heartbreaking, but it isn't the kind of desertion that Paul is speaking of in 1 Corinthians chapter 7.

This desertion is about one person deserting the vows of marriage. Not struggling to love (every spouse does that), but living in sin. It might be deserting for alcohol or for the violence of domestic abuse or for lots of things. When you are doing what you can, repenting of your sin, trying to love and respect, striving to keep your vows, but your spouse is an unchanging, manipulative, just-tell-the-pastor-the-right-thing-but-go-home-and-do-the-same-thing, then you are not bound in such circumstances. You can divorce.

Here's a huge question: How do you know? How do you know if you have God's blessing to get a divorce or if you need to bear your cross and keep working on your relationship? My answer is that you will definitely need some loving, biblical, objective assistance. When marriage goes sour, our sinful hearts are not objective. The devil lies on both sides. He convinces some of us that we can divorce when God says we can't, while persuading others of us that we can't divorce when God says we can. That's why we need each other. We need people who love God, love the Bible, love our marriage, and love us. We need people who comfort us if we're right and confront us if we're wrong. There aren't many reasons to divorce, but there are some. Together we can keep each other on God's path, the one that leads to lasting blessing.

But sadly, as you well know, not every marriage makes it. Divorce does happen. And there are reasons for you to leave in peace and move forward with God's help.

Question 3:
What about life after divorce?

I'll never forget the tears in her eyes. "Pastor, can I marry him?" She was happily engaged to a divorced man but just realized the Bible has something to say about divorced men. I give her immense credit for her question— Can I? If you were listening to Jesus and Paul, you might have wondered about that question. What if you yourself are divorced? What should you do? What if you were cheated on or deserted and ended up divorced? What if you did the cheating and deserting and divorced? What if you just ended the marriage because you both were far from happy? What options do you have that are God-approved?

Let's start with the victim of adultery or desertion. You have three options: remarry, remain single, or reconcile.

First, you could remarry. Paul said that you are not bound in such circumstances (1 Corinthians 7:15). You are free to remarry in the Lord. No stigma. No shame. God will be sitting in the first row, cheering as you say your vows.

Second, you could remain single. First Corinthians chapter 7 is a celebration of singleness and its many benefits. Singles aren't second rate. You can join Jesus and Paul and worship God with a single life, finding companionship in deep relationships with family and friends.

Third, you could reconcile. If your ex wants to and you want to, your second marriage could be a picture of God's grace. Just like God pursues his cheating bride, you could pursue her despite her infidelity. Just like Jesus takes us back after we've broken our vows yet repented, you could take him back after he sincerely desires to be a different man. Your reconciliation might remind the world of God's desire to reconcile with us.

But what if your sin ended the marriage? What if you cheated, you deserted, you filed for divorce? If that's you, God gives two commands (not options): repent and repair.

First, God commands you to repent. Hate the sin that God hates. Agree with God that your actions were wicked. Turn your back on your sin, the idol that led to desertion. Turn back to God, the God who loves to forgive wicked people.

Second, God commands you to repair. Repair what you've broken as much as possible. Produce the fruit of repentance, as John the Baptist called it. Just like a thief has to return what he took (he can't just say sorry and keep the cash), the guilty party must repair what he or she has broken. Does your ex want to be married? Then God commands you to go back. I know that might shock you, but that's what repair looks like. Go back and start a new marriage, one drastically different from the dysfunctional version you left, one with God at the center. Make your home a sanctuary, and see what God does differently this time.

Has your ex moved on? Despite your repentance and desire to do things differently, does she have no interest in a future with you? Then God commands you to live in peace even if you won't live together. Own your sin. Admit your guilt. Apologize to your ex and to Jesus. That's the "fruit" of a humble heart that is pleasing to God.

But what if you messed that up too? What if you ignored reconciliation and ran off to remarry someone else? What if, according to Jesus, you married a wrongly divorced woman? What if your wedding day was adultery in the eyes of God?

I won't lie to you, that is quite possible, especially if you didn't have a thorough understanding of the Bible's teaching on divorce and remarriage. You might need to repent today for the sins you committed in your ignorance or your stubbornness.

But here is some refreshing news: God forgives really messed-up stuff. When Jesus shouted, "It is finished!" on the cross, he meant it (John 19:30). That sin, your sin, was on his list. You were on his mind. What you have done in your relationship

God forgives really messed-up stuff.

history, no matter how unbiblical, isn't the unforgivable, you-must-carry-it-around-forever sin. You can breathe. You can go back home to your new spouse and love him or her. God wants you to stay. Even if it had a sinful start, your marriage can have a godly ending.

If you're divorced, those are your options. No matter how challenging those paths might seem, remember the promise of God: **"Trust in the LORD with all your heart. . . . In all your ways submit to him, and he will make your paths straight"** (Proverbs 3:5,6).

Question 4:
What does God think about the divorced?

Watch Jesus as he walks into Samaria. He spots the deep well outside town, finds a seat, and waits. For her. She shows up in the heat of the day, alone and ashamed, and Jesus asks her for a drink. Jesus isn't hitting on her. He's hinting to her. *Your heart is thirsty and nothing works.*

And then, in an equally cringing and compassionate moment, Jesus brings up the most sensitive part of her story—marriage. "Go, call your husband," Jesus says.

"I'm not married," she dodges. "Nope. But you're living with someone. Because the first five marriages ended in divorce, didn't they?" She changes the subject, but Jesus isn't offended. He listens. He answers. He loves. And he stays. For two days, Jesus stays in her town. He stays with her (read John 4:1–26).

What does God think about the divorced? You could ask that woman, the woman at the well, when you get to heaven. Or you could read her story here on earth. **"He had to go through Samaria"** (John 4:4). Jesus said, "I have to. There is a divorced woman in Samaria who needs me, because she needs grace." And grace is exactly what Jesus gave her.

That's the same grace that Jesus offers us, whether your marriage is a mess or you've been divorced enough times to know the county clerk by name. Christ died so there would be no second-class Chris-

Christ died so there would be no second-class Christians.

tians, no people only partially holy. **"For God so loved the world** (guess whom that includes?) **that he gave his one and only Son, that whoever** (guess whom that includes?) **believes in him shall not perish but have eternal life"** (John 3:16). Life. Never-ending life with God. Life that starts now. For the divorced. Even those divorced as often as she was.

I know that's hard to believe. If she tore you apart, spewed venom, convinced you that you were worthless. If he left, told you that you weren't good enough, not pretty enough, not worthy enough. If your dad is gone, and you wonder if God won't do the same. Listen to me. Jesus does not change. He does not vow to stay and then decide to go. He will be with you forever. He will never leave you. Never forsake you. He does not smile when you walk down the aisle and then scowl when you walk into court. His face is shining upon you, looking on you with favor. **"As a bridegroom rejoices over his bride, so will your God rejoice over you"** (Isaiah 62:5). The expression you saw on that day is the expression on God's face forever. That's what Jesus died for. So that you and I—single and divorced and dating and married and remarried—might be the bride of Christ, the beloved. So be loved. Because that's what God thinks about the divorced.

And if you are happily married, please, please, please help your repentant divorced friends not to forget God's love for them. The enemy assaults them, makes them misinterpret every sideways glance, convinces them everyone is watching, whispering, judging. So please be the one who smiles, says hello, speaks forgiveness, sets an extra spot at the dinner table. Our hurting brothers and sisters need a living, breathing reminder that they are not too damaged to be loved, to be welcomed, to be one with us. Show them what God thinks about the divorced.

In the Old Testament, God told a man named Hosea to pursue an unfaithful, immoral woman as his wife. Why would God do that? So you and I would remember that no matter what we've done, said, thought, or failed to do, we can always come home to God.

I know I haven't answered all your questions, but I deeply hope and passionately pray that God's Word, no matter what your relationship status, has filled your heart with truth and with grace.

Study Questions

1. Read Matthew 19:1–12. Find three additional points Jesus made that I did not cover in this chapter.

2. Think of three divorced people you know. How is God calling you to show them love after reading this chapter? Make a plan this week to share truth and show love to someone whose marriage has ended.

Conclusion

Husbands who lead like God. Wives who help like God. This is God's design for a good marriage. Two people become one flesh. They start a new household where he is the loving head and she is the loving helper. Both try to imitate God in their unique callings. And when they do, marriage will be so, so good. Because God makes marriage good.

When my bride and I got married, my pastor told us about the triangle of marriage. Imagine an equilateral triangle. God's at the top angle. You are at the lower left angle, and your spouse is at the lower right angle. The closer you both move to God (along the sides of the triangle), the closer you get to each other. Do you get the picture? When you are both far from God, there's tension. You don't know how much you are forgiven, so you don't know how to forgive. You don't see yourself as a messed-up sinner, so you lack patience when you realize you married one. There's sin, and there's tension.

If one of you moves closer to God, you are blessed with joy and peace, but that doesn't make a marriage that much better. She might be close to God, but that doesn't bring her closer to her spouse. But when the husband and wife draw near to God, he realizes how Jesus laid down his life for him, and he wants to lay down his preferences and say, "You first!" She realizes how God helps her every day, and she wants to say, "What can I do to help?" What happens to the tension? It releases. It turns into joy, happiness, love. Why? Because God makes marriage good.

If you're single and dating, don't forget that. You want to be close and live happily ever after. I know you do. And here's what God says will. Find someone who loves God enough to lead you in his name, to help you in his name. If you're a parent, don't forget this. Teach this to your children. Train up your child to know that a guy who lets her go to church is not good. Rather, what's good is a man who leads her to God. Because God made marriage. And it's God who makes marriage good.

So don't miss God the next time you see marriage happen. God is there, even if he didn't make the guest list. In fact, it's God's big day. When you see her walking down the aisle more beautiful than ever, there he is. That's God leading you to see how beautiful you are to him because of the blood Jesus shed on the cross. And when you see the groom fighting back tears, there he is. That's God helping you see how much he loves you despite all your flaws and sins. And when you hear how much money they sacrificed to invite you to the wedding, there he is. That's God helping you understand he sacrificed more than dollars and cents; he sacrificed all he had to make you his own. And when you feast on the free food, there he is. That's God leading you to see every good and perfect gift is free because of Jesus. Oh, everything that makes a marriage good is just a reflection of him. We shouldn't be surprised, because God made marriage. And God is the one who makes marriage good.

Notes

1. Juliana Menasce Horowitz, Nikki Graf, and Gretchen Livingston, "Marriage and Cohabitation in the U.S.," Pew Research Center, November 6, 2019, https://www.pewresearch.org/social-trends/2019/11/06/marriage-and-cohabitation-in-the-u-s/.

2. Ibid.

3. Sean Gogarty, "The Real Impact and Effectiveness of Gillette's '#metoo' ad," *MarketingWeek*, May 13, 2019, https://www.marketingweek.com/the-real-impact-and-effectiveness-of-gillettes-metoo-ad/.

4. Bruce Goldman, "Two Minds: The Cognitive Differences Between Men and Women," *Standford Medicine Magazine*, May 22, 2017, https://stanmed.stanford.edu/how-mens-and-womens-brains-are-different/.

5. Gary Shriver and Mona Shriver, *Unfaithful: Hope and Healing After Infidelity* (Colorado Springs: David C Cook, 2009), 115.

6. Ibid., 45.

About the Writer

Pastor Mike Novotny pours his Jesus-based joy into his ministry as a pastor at The CORE (Appleton, Wisconsin) and as the lead speaker for Time of Grace, a global media ministry that connects people to God through television, print, and digital resources. Unafraid to bring grace and truth to the toughest topics of our time, he has written numerous books, including *3 Words That Will Change Your Life*; *What's Big Starts Small*; *You Know God Loves You, Right?*; and *When Life Hurts*. Mike lives with his wife, Kim, and their two daughters, Brooklyn and Maya; runs long distances; and plays soccer with other middle-aged men whose best days are long behind them. To find more books by Pastor Mike, go to timeofgrace.store.

About Time of Grace

Time of Grace is an independent, donor-funded ministry that connects people to God's grace—his love, glory, and power—so they realize the temporary things of life don't satisfy. What brings satisfaction is knowing that because Jesus lived, died, and rose for all of us, we have access to the eternal God—right now and forever.

To discover more, please visit timeofgrace.org
or call 800.661.3311.

Help share God's message of grace!

Every gift you give helps Time of Grace reach people around the world with the good news of Jesus. Your generosity and prayer support take the gospel of grace to others through our ministry outreach and help them experience satisfied lives as they see God all around them.

Give today at timeofgrace.org/give
or by calling 800.661.3311.

Thank you!